DEDICATION

TO MY PURPOSE CMG AND ZPG: YOU WERE BORN FOR THIS, YOU WERE MADE FOR THIS, STRIVE FOR GREATNESS, DESTINED FOR GREATNESS!!!! YOUR TALENT WILL TAKE YOU PLACES ONLY YOUR CHARACTER CAN SUSTAIN.

TO LEG, LOVE YOU FOR YOU, MY SUN!!

TO KG & EOG, YOU ARE THE MOTIVATION, LOVE YOU!!

IN MEMORY OF CYS & NANA, YOUR LEGACY WILL LIVE ON!

MY NAME IS _____ AND I AM DETERMINED TO LIVE AN MEANINGFUL LIFE. I WILL ACT IN <u>LOVE</u>, STRIVE FOR <u>EXCELLENCE</u>, SET <u>GOALS</u>, MAINTAIN AN <u>ALL IN</u> ATTITUDE, ACT IN GOOD <u>CHARACTER</u>, AND USE MY <u>YOUTH</u> AS AN ADVANTAGE IN STARTING MY JOURNEY TO LEGACY NOW......

DATE: _____

SIGNED: _____

M & Z'S JOURNEY WITH LEGACY

KENNETH GETHERS JR

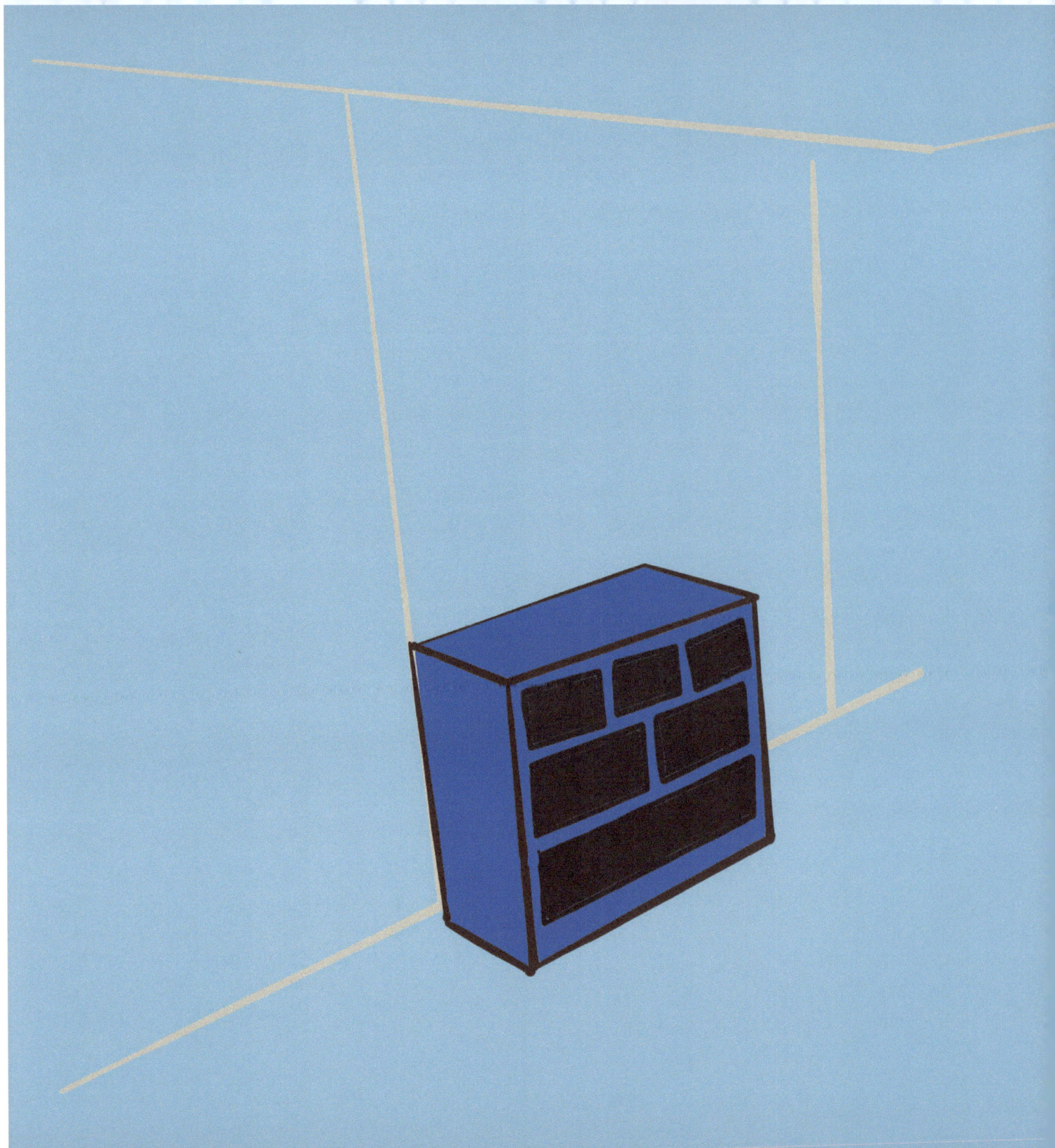

IN THE WEE HOURS OF THE MORNING, MALLOY WOKE UP TO HIS SISTER TAPPING HIM ON HIS LEG. "MALLOY, COME CHECK OUT THIS HUGE RED TRUCK SITTING IN THE LIVING ROOM," SAID ZUZU. "ZUZU, THERE IS NO TRUCK. GO BACK TO SLEEP IN YOUR ROOM," SAID MALLOY. "NO, MALLOY, TRUST ME THERE IS A BIG RED TRUCK IN THE HOUSE!" SHOUTED ZUZU. "OK ZUZU LETS GO CHECK IT OUT," SAID MALLOY.

HELLO, MALLOY AND ZUZU. MY NAME IS LEGACY, AND I'M HERE TO SHOW YOU YOUR INNER GREATNESS AND YOUR UTMOST POTENTIAL.

LEGACY MEANS ACCOMPLISHMENTS, BELIEFS AND ACTIONS YOU DEMONSTRATE IN YOUR LIVES. THAT CARRY FORWARD TO FUTURE GENERATIONS IN A WAY WHICH ALLOWS YOUR FAMILY MEMBERS, FRIENDS AND WORLD TO ADOPT AND ADAPT THEM TO MAKE THEIR LIVES MEANINGFUL.

HOP IN AND LETS ROLL!!!!

LEADERSHIP!

- HELP OTHERS
- DO NOT BE AFRAID TO BE YOURSELF

LOVE!

- LOVE WHAT YOU DO!
- LOVE YOURSELF
- YOU ARE GREAT, BEAUTIFUL / HANDSOME, MORE THAN ENOUGH

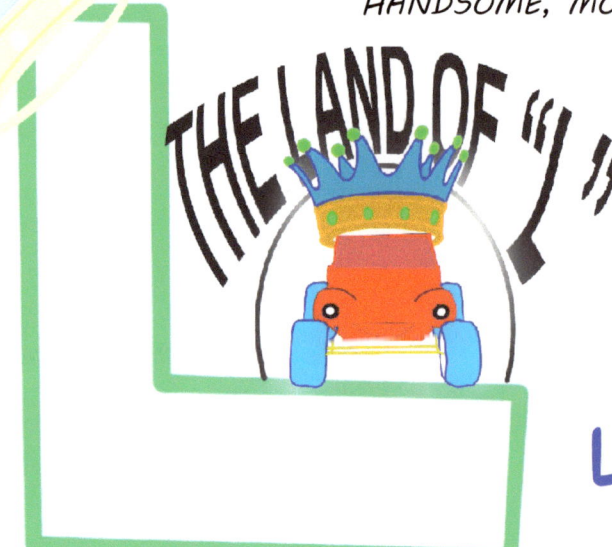

LIVE!

- YOUR PASSIONS!!
- YOUR DREAMS!!
- WHAT ARE YOU DOING TODAY, TOMORROW, NEXT YEAR TO GET THERE?

LEARN!

- READ BOOKS
- LEARN FROM YOUR MISTAKES/ EXPERIENCES.

THE PLANET OF "E"

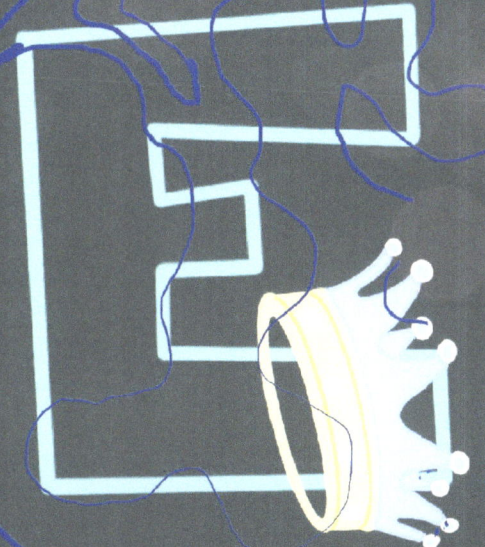

EXTRA!
- ORDINARY OR EXTRA-ORDINARY
- EXTRA TIME ON THAT HOMEWORK / ASSIGNMENT / GOAL
- EXTRA TIME STUDYING
- EXTRA TIME DISCOVERING YOUR PASSIONS, YOUR "WHY"

EXPLORE!
- EXPLORE YOUR PASSIONS / YOUR "WHY"
- TAKE A STEP IN THE UNFAMILIAR (TRUST AND BELIEVE IN YOURSELF)

WORLD OF "G"

GENERATIONS!

- GIVE BACK
- BRING VALUE AND LEAVE OPPORTUNITY FOR GROWTH

GREATNESS!

- GREATNESS LIES WITHIN YOU
- EVERYTHING THAT YOU HAVE IS EVERYTHING YOUR MISSING

GOALS!

- WRITE YOUR VISION AND MAKE IT CLEAR
- NEXT MONTH I WANT TO BE _____
- IN A YEAR I WANT TO BE _____

HOME OF "A"

AWESOME!
- YOU ARE WORTH IT
- THERE IS NO ONE LIKE YOU

ALL IN!
- DEDICATION
- COMMITMENT

ABILITY!
- YOU HAVE WHAT IT TAKES
- IF IT WERE EASY EVERYONE WOULD DO IT

FUTURE OF "C"

COLLABORATION!

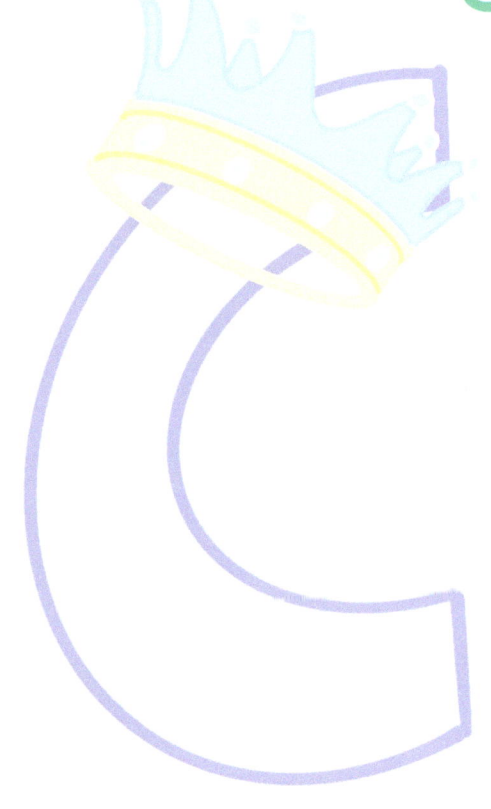

= TEAMWORK - IF YOU WANT TO GO FAST GO ALONE BUT IF YOU WANT TO GO FAR GO TOGETHER

CHARACTER!

- WHAT YOU DO WHEN NO ONE IS LOOKING

- HOW DO YOU TREAT OTHERS

- TALENT TAKES YOU PLACES ONLY YOUR CHARACTER CAN MAINTAIN

YOUTH!
- START NOW!!!
- THE WORLD NEEDS YOUR TALENT!!

Y NOT ME!
- YOU DESERVE SUCCESS
- IT BEGINS WITH YOU
- YOU DESERVE TO BE HAPPY

YEAH!
- CELEBRATE YOUR SUCCESS!!
- IT'S NOT ABOUT THE TROPHY IT IS ABOUT WHAT IT TOOK TO GRAB IT

ENDLESS MEASURE OF "Y"

MALLOY AND ZUZU WOKE UP TO BE LYING IN THE MIDDLE OF THE LIVING ROOM A MOMENT LATER. "WAS THAT A DREAM OR OUR IMAGINATION?" SHOUTED ZUZU. "NO SISTER, THAT WAS OUR DESTINY," SAID MALLOY. MALLOY GRABBED HIS SISTER'S HAND AND RAN INTO THEIR PARENT'S ROOM TO FIND THEM STILL ASLEEP, BUT THEIR BIG JUMPS HAD AWAKENED THEM.

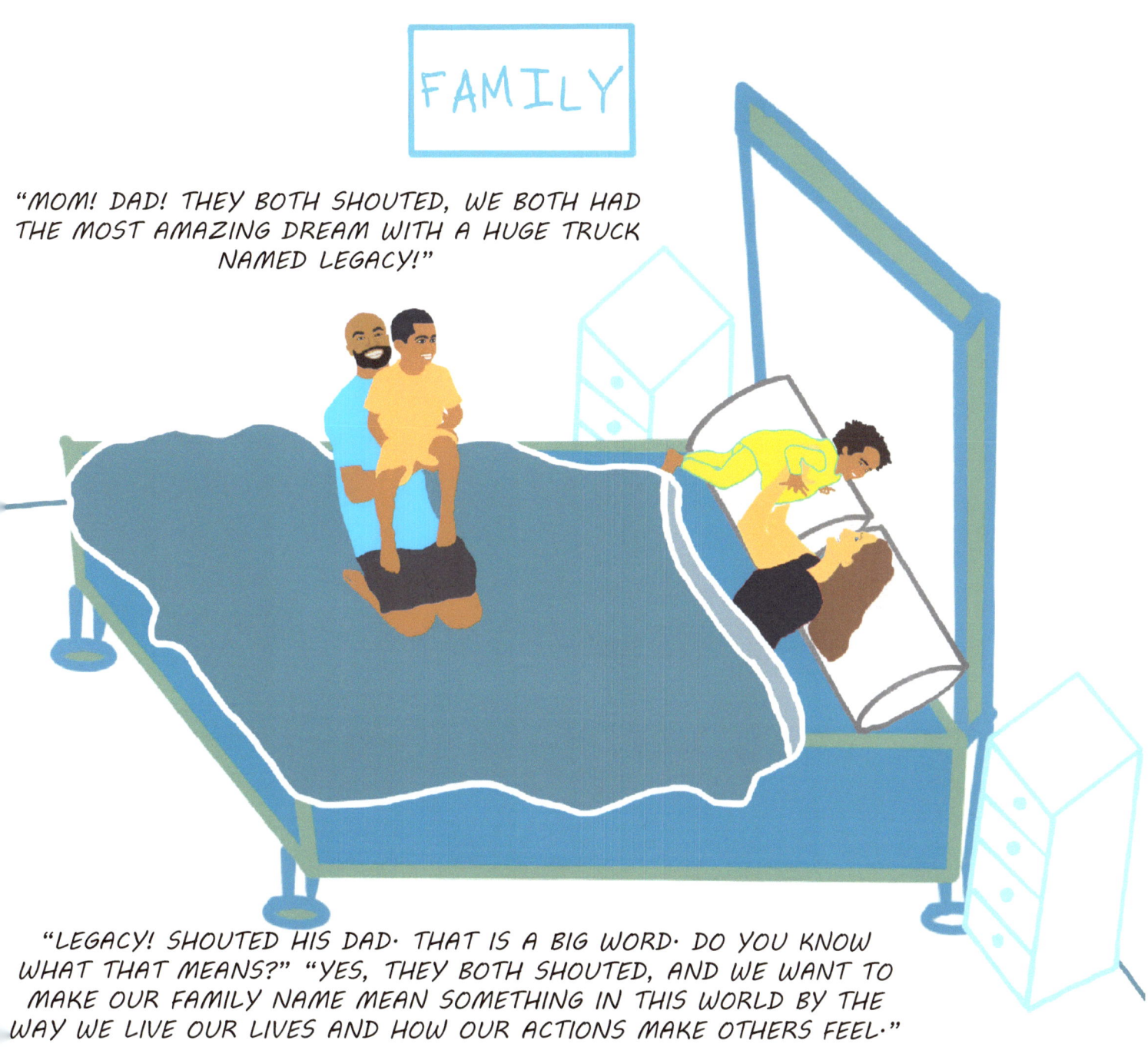

NOT THE END·····

THIS IS YOUR BEGINNING

www.ingramcontent.com/pod-product-compliance
Ingram Content Group UK Ltd.
Pitfield, Milton Keynes, MK11 3LW, UK
UKHW060125240426
12049UKWH00014B/161